Salty Sayings

from cynical tongues

Illustrated by Henry R. Martin

THE PETER PAUPER PRESS
Mount Vernon · New York

Salty Sayings

FROM CYNICAL
TONGUES

Who hunts with cats will catch but mice.

....

Public money is like holy water: everyone helps himself.

....

He that goes far to marry goes to deceive or be deceived.

He that loves glass without G, take away L and that's he.

When ill luck falls asleep, let nobody wake her.

A lucky man is rarer than a white crow.

Women only call each other sister after they have called each other a lot of other things first.

Let each man pick his own nose.

Jest with an ass, and he will slap you in the face with his tail.

You cannot ever make a crab walk straight.

A dwarf on a giant's shoulders sees farther than the giant.

It's not the skirt that ruins papa; it's the chiffon ruffles.

Glasses and lasses are brittle ware.

If all the world went naked, how could we tell the kings?

A fool and his hair are soon parted — usually in the middle.

When it is a question of money, everybody is of the same religion.

He who does not wish to become old must hang himself when young.

"A little bit goes a long way," said the wise old owl as he pooped over the precipice.

Wise men learn by others' bellyaches; fools by their own.

Make yourself a lamb and the wolves will eat you.

Drunkenness does not create vice; it merely brings it into view.

Silk was invented so that women could seem naked in clothes.

He who has no money in his purse, should have money on his tongue.

Many who pass the biggest sound, don't know their ass from a hole in the ground.

Niggard father, spendthrift son.

Money makes the old mare trot and the young tit ramble.

Love is like the measles — all the worse when it comes late in life.

Even hares pull a lion by the beard — when he is dead.

He that killeth a man when he is drunk shall be hanged when he is sober.

You can't catch old birds with chaff.

A fence between makes love more keen.

He that has no money might as well be buried in a rice tub with his mouth sewn up.

A maidenhead that laughs is half lost.

You can't sell the cow and have the milk too.

Who does not teach his child a trade brings him up to steal.

Wealth and content are not always bedfellows.

He who would eat the kernel must crack the shell.

Liquor talks mighty loud when it gets loose from the jug.

If you have the name, you may as well enjoy the game.

If you are a dog, don't be a pig too.

Money is like manure, not good unless it is spread.

An empty bag cannot stand upright.

Idle hands are the devil's tools.

He that has money may think to buy a husband for his daughter, but she may choose to sell herself cheap.

Strange! that a man who has wit enough to write a satire, should have folly enough to publish it.

You can't teach an old dog new tricks.

Pardoning the bad, is injuring the good.

A drowning man will grab the blade of a sword.

Don't send the dog to the butcher's for meat.

Money is honey, my little sonny, and a rich man's joke is always funny.

Every couple is not a pair.

He that marries for money, earns it.

He loves bacon well that licks the pig-sty door.

You cannot drink and whistle at the same time.

It takes little effort to watch a man carry a load.

The last drop makes the glass run over, and the lass fall down.

Destroy the lion while he is yet but a whelp.

It goes ill with the house when the hen sings and the cock is silent.

Wealth is not his that has it, but his that enjoys it.

Clean your finger, before you point at another's spots.

A mouse, in time, may bite in two a great cable.

Money is the best bait when you go a-fishing for men.

A hypocrite fawns with the tail and bites with the mouth.

If Jack's in love, he's no judge of Jill's beauty.

Waste no water on a drowned mouse.

The worst life is better than the best possible death.

Cut off the dog's tail, but he remains a dog.

He that serves God for money will serve the devil for more of the same.

The devil wipes his breech with poor folks' pride.

There are three faithful friends — an old wife, an old dog, and ready money.

The hasty bitch brings forth blind puppies.

All wish to possess life, but few are willing to pay the price.

He that waits for chance is never sure of his dinner.

One eye of the master's sees more than ten of the servants'.

Virtue may not always make a face handsome, but vice will certainly make it ugly.

The art of the merchant lies more in getting paid than in making sales.

Do not ask a blind man which is the right way.

The miser and the pig are of no use to the family till dead.

An ass laden with gold can enter the gates of the city.

In married life three is company and two is none.

Mellow nuts have the hardest rind.

A man is as old as he feels; a woman as old as she looks.

To be intimate with a foolish friend, is like going to bed with a razor.

I can resist everything except temptation.

An army, like a serpent, goes on its belly.

A beard breeds lice, not wisdom.

He that makes himself an ass, must not take it ill if men ride him.

Draw the snake out of the hole with another's hand.

A dog will not cry if you beat him with a bone.

The higher the baboon climbs, the more he shows his butt.

One good husband is worth two good wives; the scarcer things are, the more they're valued.

It's a lazy dog that leans against a wall to bark.

―――――――――――――――

Apes are never more beasts than when they wear men's clothes.

―――――――――――――――

The doctor is more to be feared than the disease.

The day of the miser's death is the heir's holiday.

Office without pay makes thieves.

Silence is not always a sign of wisdom, but babbling is ever a folly.

What cures Morris makes Martha sick indeed nine months after.

A good archer is not known by his arrow but by his aim.

He that mischief hatcheth, mischief catcheth.

Every ass loves to hear himself bray.

Two cats in one bag cannot have peace.

The dog's kennel is not the place to store sausage.

Every dog returns to his own vomit.

There is no eel so small but it hopes to become a whale.

The king's cheese goes half to waste in parings.

Oh! how many torments lie in the small circle of a wedding ring!

When there is an old maid in the house, a watch dog is unnecessary.

When Bacchus pokes the fire, Venus smiles by the oven.

The mirror shows everyone his best friend.

An ass is beautiful to an ass, and a pig to a pig.

There are cheaper ways of killing a cat than choking her with cream.

Observe the mother before you take the daughter.

What the law demands, give of your own free will.

Needles and pins, needles and pins; when a man marries, his trouble begins.

One man's meat is another man's poison.

A baby is an angel whose wings decrease as his legs increase.

A hair of the dog cures the bite.

A thistle is a fine salad for an ass' mouth.

A careless mother throws the child out with the bath.

Often while the doctors consult, the patient dies.

Better be the head of an ass than the ass of a horse.

Love is like linen: often changed, the sweeter.

It is a foolish dog that bites the stone instead of him that throws it.

The ugly spinster loves the minister.

An oath and an egg are soon broken.

There is more to marriage than four bare legs in a bed.

A piece of a kid is worth two of a cat.

There's no use trying to get blood out of a turnip.

If you want a thing done, go; if not, send.

When a dog is drowning, everyone offers him a drink.

The cards are ill shuffled till I have a good hand.

21

If the doctor cures, the sun sees it; if he kills, the earth hides it.

Marry your son when you will, your daughter when you can.

A black hen can lay a white egg.

The devil lies brooding in the miser's chest.

The hook without bait catches no fish; no friends come to an empty dish.

The last barker is the first biter.

A man in a passion rides a mad horse.

In dance the hand hath liberty to touch.

Every man likes the smell of his own excrement.

Fools bite one another, but wise men agree.

He that hath a full purse never wanted a friend.

Blessed be poverty — when the tax-collector cometh.

Marriage has many pains, but celibacy has no pleasures.

Next to the pleasure of taking a new mistress is that of being rid of an old one.

A greedy man would drive a louse for its fur and fat to the slaughterhouse.

Everyone bastes the fat dog, while the lean one burns.

To be proud of virtue, is to poison yourself with the antidote.

One doctor makes work for another.

Curses, like chickens, come home to roost.

23

He's the best physician that knows the worthlessness of most medicines.

To love oneself is the beginning of a lifelong romance.

He that hath a head of wax must not walk in the sun.

Every door may be shut but death's.

Not even a thousand men in armor can strip a naked man.

A lock is made only for the honest man; the thief will break it.

The last straw breaks the camel's back, the last bean splits the strongest sack.

Even the lion must defend himself against gnats.

Bachelors' wives and maids' children are well behaved.

The greatest king must at last go to bed with a shovel.

Learn of the skillful: he that teaches himself, hath a fool for his master.

He that drinks his cider alone, let him catch his horse alone.

Better the devil you know than the devil you don't know.

There are no ugly loves, nor handsome prisons.

A bad tree does not yield good apples.

Fools they are a funny race: they cut off their nose to spite their face.

A poor man who marries a wealthy woman gets a ruler and not a wife.

Don't make yourself a mouse, or the cat will eat you.

A living invalid knows more than a dead doctor.

Samson, for all his strong body, had a weak head, or he would not have laid it in a harlot's lap.

The calmest husbands make the stormiest wives.

A curse will not strike out an eye unless a fist goes with it.

Man's tongue is soft, and bone doth lack; yet a stroke therewith may break a man's back.

If youth but knew, if old age could!

Scabby heads love not the comb.

Lovers live by love as larks live by leeks.

A golden key opens many a stubborn lock.

Cleopatra's nose: had it been shorter, the aspect of the whole world would have been changed.

Many a good hanging would prevent a bad marriage.

First the belly carries the legs, and then the legs the belly.

The tongue offends, and the ears get the cuffing.

There is no better companion than a fat wallet.

Thousands drink themselves to death before one dies of thirst.

Into the mouth of a bad dog often falls a good bone.

Better a snotty child than his nose worn off by wiping.

Light-heeled mothers make heavy-heeled daughters.

The poor man must walk to get meat for his stomach, the rich man to get stomach for his meat.

The ass that brays most eats least.

Keep the eyes wide open before marriage, and half shut afterwards.

A fox should be excused from the jury at the trial of a goose.

The mouth is not sweetened by saying, "Honey, honey."

Give up all hope of peace so long as your mother-in-law lives.

Misfortunes, wood, and hair grow throughout the year.

The rotten apple spoils his companions.

Though the mastiff be gentle, yet bite him not by the lip.

When the boy is growing he has a wolf in his belly.

A dead mouse feels no cold.

No one can boast of his modesty.

You can go far with a lie, but you can't come back.

Many foxes grow grey, but few grow good.

An old man is a bed full of bones.

A keen head is rarely set on a fat belly.

Nobody wants to kiss first when he is hungry.

Write with the learned, pronounce with the vulgar.

Vice knows she's ugly, so she puts on her painted mask.

To the boiling pot the flies come not.

A man who desires to get married should know either everything or nothing.

A woman, an ass, and a walnut tree, they bring the more fruit, the more beaten they be.

The money paid, the work delayed.

Better go to heaven in rags than to hell in embroidery.

The difference is wide that a double bed will not decide.

It is too late for the bird to scream when he is caught.

The worst wheel of the cart makes the most noise.

Marry above thy match, and thou wilt get a master.

An old man has the almanac in his body.

A fatherless child is half an orphan; a motherless child, a whole orphan.

When a mother calls her own child "bastard!" — you may believe her.

An old lion is better than a young ass, and more to be feared.

When a dog bites a man, that is not news. When a man bites a dog, that's news.

Hope makes the fool rich.

If you haven't capon in the pot, feed on an onion, and beweep your lot.

A bustling mother makes a slothful daughter.

A husband's handcuffs leave no mark on his wrist.

You can't make an omelet without breaking some eggs.

There's more old drunkards, than old doctors.

You cannot pluck roses without fear of thorns, nor enjoy a fair wife without danger of horns.

A greased mouth cannot say no.

A crown is no cure for the headache.

Seven wealthy towns contend for Homer dead, through which the living Homer begged his bread.

A mother needs a large apron to cover her children's faults.

Under the blanket the black one is as good as the white.

He runs from the bear to fall in with the wolves.

He who comes late must eat what is left.

Lips, however rosy, must be fed.

You must have iron nails if you want to go scratching with a bear.

He that wipes the child's nose kisses the mother's cheek.

The weeping of the heirs is only laughter masked.

Children suck the mother when they are young, and the father when they are old.

34

Look not for musk in a dog's kennel.

A happy couple: the husband deaf, the wife blind.

If a maid marries an old man, he can expect to leave a young widow.

The rich miser and the fat goat are good only after they are dead.

One foot is better than two crutches.

A mob is a monster with many hands and no brains.

Never take a wife till thou hast a house (and a fire) to put her in.

What is born of a cat will catch mice.

The black crow thinks her own birds white.

If you'd lose a troublesome visitor, lend him money.

There is nobody will go to hell for company.

When the wolf comes in at the door, love flies out at the window.

So live that you can look any man in the eye and tell him to go to hell.

I'll laugh and be fat, for care killed a cat.

He who listens at doors hears much more than he likes.

He was a bold man indeed that first ate an oyster.

Teach your child to hold his tongue; he'll learn fast enough to speak.

One mother can take care of ten children, but ten children can't take care of one mother.

Modest dogs miss much meat.

Marriage halves our joys, doubles our expenses, and quadruples our tempers.

Beggars breed and rich men feed.

Books are bad crutches, but good walking-sticks.

Ask advice, but use your own common sense in taking it.

If the beard were all, a goat might preach.

All are not hunters that blow the horn.

The virtuous maid and the broken leg must stay at home.

To beg of the miser is to dig a trench in the sea.

He that falls in love with himself, will have no rivals.

Life's a long headache in a noisy street.

He's a fool that makes his doctor his heir.

When man and woman die, as poets sung, his heart's the last part moves; her last, the tongue.

Crows are never the whiter for washing themselves.

The price of your hat isn't the measure of your brain.

As a man grows older, he oft grows colder.

Happy is she who marries the son of a dead mother.

Fish, Penelope, or cut bait!

Bees that have honey in their mouths have stings in their tails.

A man is as good as he has to be; a woman as bad as she dares.

A hiccup is the laughter of a fool.

Better a louse in the pot than no flesh at all.

Elbow grease gives the best polish.

Love never dies of starvation, but often of indigestion.

Everything helps, quoth the wren, when she pissed into the sea.

There is small choice in rotten apples.

Who would not be deceived must have as many eyes as hairs on his head.

The hawk kissed the hen — up to the last feather.

If man could have half his wishes, he would double his troubles.

The deaf man heard the dumb man say that the blind man saw the lame man run.

Old boys have their playthings as well as young ones; the difference is only in the price.

The cure, my son, may be far worse than the disease.

A critic is a legless man who teaches running.

Only the foolish and the dead never change their opinions.

Bore: a person who talks when you want him to listen.

Don't think to hunt two hares with one dog.

It's a bad hen that eats at your house and lays at another's.

The smallest insect may cause death by its bite.

Heaven help the sheep when the wolf is judge.

Make sure of the bear before you sell his skin.

The greater the fool the smoother the dancer.

The sting of a reproach is the truth of it.

Three may keep a secret, if two of them are dead.

He who peeps through a hole may see what will vex him.

Neither a fortress nor a maidenhead will hold out long after they begin to parley.

God heals and the doctor takes the fee.

Every herring must hang by its own gill.

Long engagements give people the opportunity of finding out each other's character before marriage, which is never advisable.

Better to beg than steal, but better to work than beg.

They love dancing well that dance barefoot upon thorns.

The tongue of women is their sword; they take care not to let it rust.

A handsome hostess makes a dear reckoning.

The cat in gloves catches no mice.

If ignorance is bliss how silly to borrow your neighbor's newspaper!

Who sells on credit has much business but little cash.

The doctor can cure the sick, but he cannot cure the dead.

Every heart hath its own ache.

The woman who hesitates is lost.

An Irishman never speaks well of another Irishman.

Bed is a married man's medicine and a bachelor's delight.

An old man dancing is a child in mind and heart.

The fool jumps into the water for fear of the rain.

Fear the goat from the front, the horse from the rear, and man from all sides.

He who can lick can bite.

Necessity makes an honest man a knave.

A lewd bachelor makes a jealous husband.

Judges should have two ears, both alike.

When it rains porridge the beggar always discovers he has no spoon.

Six feet of earth make all men equal.

The mother knows best whether the child is like the father.

Write injuries in dust, benefits in marble.

Why so flushed? — I want to get married. Why so pale? — I am married.

He who marries for love without money has good nights and sorry days.

If your friend takes off the cream, what remains is sour milk.

The kick of the dam hurts not the colt.

He who goes to law for a sheep loses his cow.

The tongue ever turns to the aching tooth.

He that does you an ill turn will never forgive you.

Don't praise marriage on the third day, but after the third year.

Where there's marriage without love, there will be love without marriage.

The surest way to hit a woman's heart is to take aim kneeling.

It is difference of opinion that makes horse-races.

What can you expect from a hog but a grunt?

History is lies agreed upon.

He who spares the bad, ends by corrupting the good.

A lean compromise is better than a fat lawsuit.

A beggar's estate lies in many lands.

Pretty maids and dead fish do not keep.

An open door may tempt a saint.

The prodigal son who returns for the inheritance, often has to pay the funeral expenses.

No pot so ugly but finds its cover.

Dispute the price but don't dispute the weight.

48

To win the mistress, first bribe the maid.

The empty belly hates a long sermon.

When death puts out the flame, the snuff will tell if we are wax or tallow, by the smell.

To get married is to tie a knot with the tongue that you can't undo with your teeth.

A pretty pig makes an ugly hog.

Kings and bears often worry their keepers.

Few lawyers die well, few physicians live well.

Who has a bad name is half hanged.

Two daughters and a back door, do spoil your sleep forever more.

Opportunity makes the thief.

Better a finger off than aye wagging.

Orators are driven by their weakness to noise, as lame men take to horses.

He that is his own lawyer has a fool for his client.

Every cock crows on his own dung-hill.

He that eats the king's goose shall be choked with his feathers.

If there were no bad people there would be no good lawyers.

What avails it to have our bellies full of meat if it be not digested?

He that deals in dirt has foul fingers.

All is not butter that comes from the cow.

Though women are angels yet, wed-lock's the devil.

Save a thief from the gallows, and he will cut your throat.

He who boasts of his descent is like the potato; the best part of him is under ground.

A drop of honey catches more flies than a barrel of vinegar.

A pouting miss is good to kiss.

Lawyers' houses are built with the hollow heads of fools.

The best pears fall into the pig's mouth.

The hog you buy on credit grunts till he's paid for.

One had as good eat the devil as the broth he's boiled in.

If a man deceives me once, shame on him; if he deceives me twice, shame on me.

We desire nothing so much as what we ought not to have.

A miser's heart is as cold as a witch's tit.

Better to sit up all night than go to bed with a dragon.

What in the great is called liberty, in the little is called license.

Dry bread with love is better than a fat capon with fear.

The louder he talked of his honor, the faster we counted our spoons.

Better a poor horse than an empty stall.

To marry once is a duty, twice a folly, thrice is madness.

If lies were Latin, there would be many learned men.

He that lies down with dogs will rise up with fleas.

A man must make himself despicable before he is despised.

An honest man does not make himself a dog for the sake of a bone.

Better keep the devil at the door than turn him out of the house.

Milk the cow but don't pull off the teats.

One scabbed sheep will taint a whole flock.

Second marriage is the triumph of hope over experience.

Better ride a lame horse than go afoot.

A poor man between two lawyers is like a fish between two cats.

Better half an egg than an empty shell.

A deceitful man cries wine and sells vinegar.

A pig that has two owners is sure to die of hunger.

Three Philadelphia lawyers are a match for the devil.

He who goes with wolves will learn to howl.

The mouse does not leave the cat's house with a full belly.

A closed mouth catches no flies.

To whom God gave no sons, the devil gives nephews.

He who wants a mule without fault must walk on foot.

A lazy boy and a warm bed are difficult to part.

If two men ride on a horse, one must ride behind.

Man is the only animal that blushes, or needs to.

Spice a dish with love, and it pleases every palate.

A diplomat is a man who remembers a woman's birthday and forgets her age.

Three women and a goose make a market.

Many do kiss the child for love of the nurse.

He must have a long spoon that will eat with the devil.

Choose your wife by ear rather than by eye.

Calf love, half love; old love, cold love.

Man is a little soul carrying around a big corpse.

He who is full of himself, is likely to be quite empty.

In the kingdom of the blind, the one-eyed man is king.

A bore is a man who, when you ask him how he is, tells you.

A pebble and a diamond are alike to a blind man.

Advice to those about to marry — Don't.

Every woman should marry, and no man.

Courting and wooing bring dallying and doing.

The man who has no courage should have fast legs.

Kissing don't last: cookery do.

The flea and the louse are the beggar's most loyal companions.

Good breeding consists in concealing how much we think of ourselves and how little we think of others.

It is the sick oyster which nurtures the pearl.

In old houses many mice, in old furs many lice.

The old man who marries bids Death to the feast.

Ill luck comes by pounds and goes away by ounces.

The coat is new; only the holes are old.

The cowl does not make the monk.

The sleeping fox catches no poultry.

To lose your mind you must have a mind to lose.

Those who never had a cushion don't miss it.

A mad beast must have a sober driver.

Better coarse clothing than naked thighs.

A cynic is a man who knows the price of everything, and the value of nothing.

The miser is always poor.

Women are not much, but they are the best other sex we have.